UNEXPLAINED

Rupert Matthews

QEB Publishing

Project Editor: Paul Manning/White-Thomson Publishing
Designer: Tim Mayer/White-Thomson Publishing
Picture Researcher: Maria Joannou

A CIP record for this book is available from the Library of Congress.

ISBN 978-1-59566-845-5

Printed in Guangdong, China

10 9 8 7 6 5 4 3 2 1

The words in **bold**
are explained in the
glossary on page 60.

You can find the answers to
the questions asked on these
notebooks on page 62.

CONTENTS

BOWMEN

≈ AND OTHER LEGENDS OF THE WAR

BY ARTHUR MACHEN

SIMPKIN, MARSHALL, HAMILTON, KENT

GHOSTS

For centuries, people all over the world have told stories about ghosts. Some argue that ghosts are nothing but fantasy. But others firmly believe that ghosts are real. Read these pages and decide for yourself.

FACT OR FICTION?

Many ghost stories turn out to have a simple explanation. For example, a house in the city of Bath in the UK was said to be haunted by the sound of a piano playing, until it was found that the ghostly music came from a piano two houses away. The sound was carried by the water pipes!

 Borley Rectory in Essex was once known as the most haunted house in England.

HOAXES

Sometimes ghosts turn out to be **hoaxes**, or tricks. More often, they are the result of **hallucinations**, when people see or hear things that are not really there. But not all ghost **sightings** can be explained so easily.

INVESTIGATOR'S ESSENTIALS

Among the tools used by ghost hunters and paranormal investigators are:

Camera — to take photos and movies

Recorder — to record unusual sounds

EMF detector — to measure changes in **electromagnetic** energy

Thermometer — to measure changes in temperature

Notebook — to record the time, place, and other details of paranormal activity

 Victorian photographers often claimed to have captured ghosts on film. This photograph was believed to show a man being visited by the spirit of his dead wife. It was later exposed as a fake.

GHOST HUNTERS

When a witness claims to have seen a ghost clearly and at close range, ghost hunters or **paranormal** investigators will sometimes interview them and try to find out more. Often they will use cameras and special equipment to gather information about the ghost. If there isn't a scientific explanation, the ghost hunters treat the sighting as **genuine**.

 Harry Price (1881–1948) was one of the best-known ghost hunters of his time and carried out many famous investigations of haunted houses.

7

THE LINCOLN GHOST

A "classic ghost" always appears in the same place and behaves in the same way. Most classic ghosts are **apparitions** of people who have died some time ago. Sometimes they are even mistaken for real people.

INTO THIN AIR

During World War II, British Prime Minister Winston Churchill was staying in the White House as a guest of U.S. President Franklin D. Roosevelt. As he was dressing for dinner in the Lincoln Bedroom one evening, he became aware of a tall figure wearing a dark suit standing in the room.

Startled, Churchill said, "You have me at a disadvantage, Sir!" The man smiled and then vanished into thin air. Churchill later identified the ghost as that of President Abraham Lincoln.

GHOST FILE

Subject   Abraham Lincoln
Sighting   May 19, 1943
Place   The White House, Washington DC, USA
Status   UNEXPLAINED

 The White House in Washington D.C. is the official home of U.S. presidents.

Abraham Lincoln, born in 1809, was president of the USA from 1861 until 1865, when he was assassinated during a visit to the theater.

FACT OR FANTASY?

When Queen Wilhelmina of the Netherlands stayed at the White House in 1948, she was awakened in the night by a knock on the door. When she answered it, she saw Lincoln's ghost staring at her from the hallway. She fainted and woke up later to find herself lying on the floor of her room.

Grace Coolidge, wife of U.S. President Calvin Coolidge (1872–1933), often reported seeing the Lincoln ghost.

WHITE HOUSE WITNESSES

Churchill was not the first or last to see the Lincoln ghost. Other witnesses included Franklin Roosevelt's wife, Eleanor, and Maureen Reagan, daughter of U.S. President Ronald Reagan (1911–2004). The Reagans' dog apparently refused to enter the Lincoln bedroom and often stood outside the door barking.

WHAT HAPPENED NEXT?

After each sighting, the White House was thoroughly searched for intruders, but none were ever found. Since 1947, there has only been one sighting of the Lincoln ghost, but ghostly sounds are still heard in the White House to this day.

Who fainted after meeting the White House ghost?

When did President Lincoln die?

What did Winston Churchill say to the ghost?

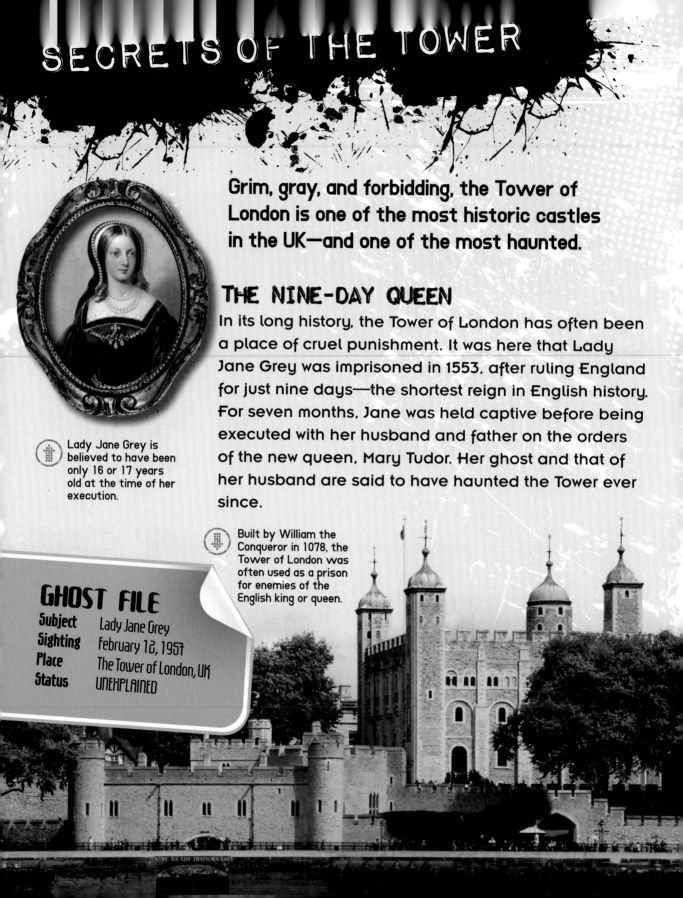

Grim, gray, and forbidding, the Tower of London is one of the most historic castles in the UK—and one of the most haunted.

THE NINE-DAY QUEEN

In its long history, the Tower of London has often been a place of cruel punishment. It was here that Lady Jane Grey was imprisoned in 1553, after ruling England for just nine days—the shortest reign in English history. For seven months, Jane was held captive before being executed with her husband and father on the orders of the new queen, Mary Tudor. Her ghost and that of her husband are said to have haunted the Tower ever since.

Lady Jane Grey is believed to have been only 16 or 17 years old at the time of her execution.

Built by William the Conqueror in 1078, the Tower of London was often used as a prison for enemies of the English king or queen.

GHOST FILE

Subject Lady Jane Grey
Sighting February 12, 1957
Place The Tower of London, UK
Status UNEXPLAINED

NTRY TO THE TRAITORS GATE

GHOSTS OF HISTORY

Many other historical figures are said to stalk the gloomy nooks and crannies of the Tower. The wife of Henry VIII, Anne Boleyn, who was beheaded on Tower Hill in 1536, has been seen in the Chapel. Sir Walter Raleigh, executed in 1618, is said to haunt the Bloody Tower. The white-clad figures of two small boys, said to be the murdered nephews of Richard III, have also been seen there.

FACT OR FANTASY?

One evening in 1957, two Tower of London guards saw the strange misty figure of a woman in a long dress walking on the battlements. After several paces, the figure disappeared. The sighting took place on February 12—the exact date of the execution of Lady Jane Grey in 1554.

These two young nephews of Richard III are among the ghosts that are said to haunt the Bloody Tower.

Where was the ghost of Lady Jane Grey seen in 1957?

Who was Anne Boleyn's husband?

Who are the two small boys who haunt the Bloody Tower?

CRIES AND WHISPERS

With its echoing **flagstone** floors, gloomy corridors, and gruesome exhibits, it is hard to imagine a creepier place than Old Melbourne Gaol in Australia.

 Cries of long-dead prisoners and sounds of ghostly footsteps are said to echo down the corridors of Old Melbourne Gaol.

 The **death mask** of Ned Kelly is one of many grisly items on display at the prison.

PRISON GHOSTS

Built in 1841, Melbourne Gaol (pronounced "jail") once housed hundreds of Australia's most dangerous criminals, including the outlaw Ned Kelly. He was hung in 1880. Between 1841 and 1924, more than 130 prisoners were executed, and many are said to haunt the Gaol today. Whether or not the tales are true, you certainly feel a shiver when you step inside.

SHADOWY FIGURES

Since the prison was turned into a museum in 1972, there have been countless reports of ghostly figures, strange noises, and glowing lights. Many visitors have also spoken of feeling a sudden mysterious chill in the atmosphere.

One ghost believed to haunt Melbourne Gaol is that of prisoner "Lucy R," who committed suicide in 1865. Ghost hunters who spent a night in the prison on the anniversary of her death even claim to have recorded her voice crying for help from Cell 16.

When was Old Melbourne Gaol built?

Which famous outlaw was executed there in 1880?

When did the prison become a museum?

FACT OR FANTASY?

One night, the museum's curator was working late in his office when he heard footsteps, followed by scratching at his door. Stepping outside, he found the corridor deserted. No wonder he prefers to work when there are people around!

 Hangings took place on this first floor landing where a trapdoor, known as the Hangman's Box, was cut into the floor.

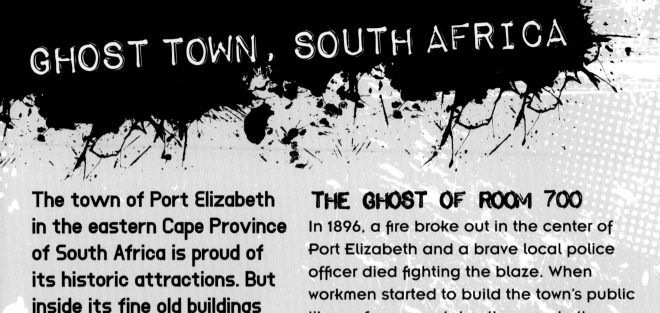

GHOST TOWN, SOUTH AFRICA

The town of Port Elizabeth in the eastern Cape Province of South Africa is proud of its historic attractions. But inside its fine old buildings lurk a host of ghosts and phantoms...

THE GHOST OF ROOM 700

In 1896, a fire broke out in the center of Port Elizabeth and a brave local police officer died fighting the blaze. When workmen started to build the town's public library five years later, they made the mistake of removing Officer Maxwell's **memorial** from the site. For years after, his angry ghost was said to haunt the building. Happily, when the memorial was returned, the ghost of Room 700 was seen no more!

Scary apparitions, doors slamming shut for no reason, and books flying through the air have all been reported at Port Elizabeth's spooky public library.

FACT OR FANTASY?

One old house in Port Elizabeth is said to be haunted by the spirit of a young servant girl who was murdered by her boyfriend. The girl had the task of dusting the piano. People who lived there later claim to have heard ghostly music floating from the drawing room.

RESTLESS SPIRITS

Supernatural activity in a building is often linked to violent or tragic events that took place there, such as a murder, accidental death, or suicide. Many hauntings are also said to be due to "restless spirits"—ghosts who are sad or angry because their remains or final resting place have been disturbed.

BANGING DOORS

Another person said to haunt the Port Elizabeth library is its former **caretaker.** For 31 years, Robert Thomas devoted himself to looking after the building. Even today, he still goes around, banging doors, stacking books—and sometimes throwing them across the room!

GHOST FILE

Subject	Robert Thomas, caretaker
Sightings	Several since 1943
Place	Port Elizabeth Library, South Africa
Status	UNEXPLAINED

The entrance of Port Elizabeth's fine Victorian public library.

Where is Port Elizabeth?

Who was the ghost of Room 700?

Whose ghost still haunts the library?

THE "ANGELS OF MONS"

Some tales of ghosts and the **supernatural** seem so far-fetched, it is hard to believe that people once thought they were true. One such tale is the "Angels of Mons."

MIRACLE RESCUE

On April 24, 1915, at the height of World War I, a bizarre story appeared in the pages of a British magazine. It described how a supernatural force of "angels" had **miraculously** rescued a group of British soldiers during the Battle of Mons, Belgium, in August 1914.

GHOST FILE

Subject	The "Angels of Mons"
Sighting	August 1914
Place	Mons, Belgium
Status	DISPROVED

The story quickly spread. Suddenly, everybody was talking about the "Angels of Mons." According to the newspapers, even soldiers who had fought in the battle were saying the story was true!

Soldiers who fought in the trenches during World War I saw terrible sights that often haunted them for their rest of their lives.

BIRTH OF A LEGEND

In fact, it all began with the British writer Arthur Machen. His story "The Bowmen," published the year before, told how British troops at Mons had been helped by ghostly English archers from the Battle of Agincourt, France, in 1415. The story was meant to make people feel proud and patriotic—but it was never based on a real event.

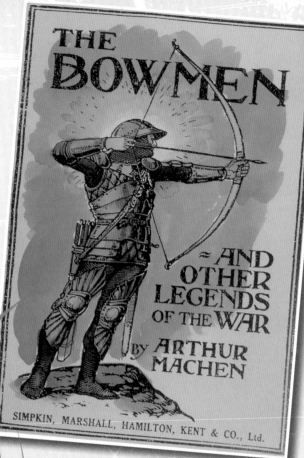

THE BOWMEN ≈AND OTHER LEGENDS OF THE WAR BY ARTHUR MACHEN

SIMPKIN, MARSHALL, HAMILTON, KENT & CO., Ltd.

FACT OR FANTASY?

The only evidence for the "Angels" story came from a group of Irish Guards who became lost during the battle and were helped to safety by a woman with a lamp. There is no reason to believe the woman was a ghost, but her rescue of the soldiers may have helped spread the "Angels" legend.

Embarrassed by the spread of the "Angels" **legend**, Arthur Machen always insisted his "Bowmen" story was just a work of **fiction**.

WHAT HAPPENED NEXT?

When Machen realized that he had started all the talk about "angels," he was horrified. He tried to explain that his story was made up, but nobody would listen. In the end, the story was repeated so often, everybody came to believe it was true.

What battle took place in Belgium in August 1914?

When did the story of the "Angels of Mons" first appear?

Who wrote the story "The Bowmen?"

THE FLYING DUTCHMAN

According to legend, the ghostly ship known as the Flying Dutchman was doomed to sail the seas forever, bringing death and disaster to all who saw her. Amazingly, this scary story is partly based on fact.

GHOST FILE

Subject   Flying Dutchman
Date   1676
Sighting   Indian Ocean
Status   UNEXPLAINED

WILD STORIES

The real-life *Flying Dutchman* was a seventeenth-century sailing ship owned by a captain named Van der Decken. When the ship vanished in a storm off the coast of South Africa in 1676, many wild stories were told about her.

Some said that a dreadful crime had been committed on board. Others said that the crew had been struck down with plague. Many believed that the ship was **cursed** because the captain had made a **pact** with the Devil.

This famous painting by William Wyllie shows sailors abandoning ship after meeting the ghostly *Flying Dutchman* on the high seas.

MYSTERY SHIP

In 1880, the future King George V of England was sailing to Sydney, Australia, on board the Royal Navy vessel, the HMS Bacchante. At 4 A.M. one day, the lookout spotted a glowing-red sailing ship on the horizon. Mysteriously, as the ghostly ship drew nearer, it suddenly vanished into thin air.

 George V always had a love of the sea and served in the Royal Navy before becoming king of England in 1910.

FACT OR FANTASY?

Tales of ghost ships are not uncommon. According to local folklore, the Caleuche is a ghost ship which sails the seas at night around Chiloé Island, off the coast of Chile. Witnesses speak of hearing music and laughter from on board, before the beautiful ship once again disappears into the night.

WHAT HAPPENED NEXT?

Later that day, a terrible accident took place on board. The seaman who had spotted the mystery ship fell from the rigging and was found lying dead on the **forecastle** deck.

After this, the future King firmly believed the ghost ship seen that day was the *Flying Dutchman*. Could it be true?

When did the *Flying Dutchman* disappear?

Who was the captain of the *Flying Dutchman*?

Which British king claimed to have seen the *Flying Dutchman*?

THE GHOST GIRL OF CUCUTA

Occasionally, people invent ghosts to try to fool others. But few invented ghosts have fooled as many people as the ghost girl of Cucuta!

THE GIRL IN WHITE

In May 2007, the Colombian television station RCN showed a film about a ghost that was said to haunt the town of Cucuta in northeast Colombia. The ghost was of a 12-year-old girl who had been murdered in a local park 30 years before. The film included interviews with eyewitnesses, and even video clips showing a sinister white figure gliding through the park at night.

When the film was shown, it caused a sensation. Soon viewers started calling in to say that they had seen the ghost, too!

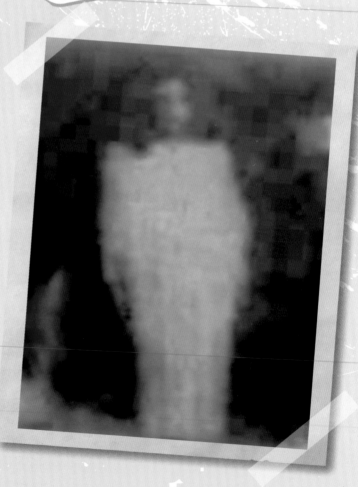

This shot of a ghostly white figure was said to have been taken in Villa Camila Park in Cucuta.

FACT OR FANTASY?

The Cucuta "ghost girl" hoax depended on clever special effects and camera tricks, but also on convincing performances by the "witnesses." Interviews with people who claimed to have seen the ghost—including a local priest —all made the story seem more believable.

 Interviews with witnesses made the "ghost girl" story seem very convincing.

WHAT HAPPENED NEXT?

A year later, a Colombian website revealed the truth. The "ghost" was a hoax created by a television news team. The interviews with "witnesses" were faked. The "ghost" shown in the film was a projection of a photograph of a girl taken at a **fiesta** in 2005.

Which TV channel showed the film of the "ghost?"

In which park was the "ghost" seen?

How was the "ghost" created?

 This clip of the ghost gliding through the park at night looks very realistic. Would you have been fooled?

21

THE BELL WITCH

During the early 1800s, the "Bell Witch" was the most famous ghost in the USA. The story of how the vengeful spirit of an old woman terrorized a Tennessee farmer and his family is among the most chilling tales of the supernatural ever told.

This picture of Betsy Bell in the grip of the poltergeist comes from one of the many books about the Bell Witch legend.

GHOST FILE

Subject	The Bell Witch
Date	1817–1820
Sighting	The Bell Farm, Adams, Tennessee, USA
Status	UNEXPLAINED

AN UNSEEN FORCE

The haunting began in 1817, when John Bell first noticed strange-looking animals around his farm. Soon afterward, the family began to hear violent knocking, bumping, and gnawing sounds around the house. At the same time, Betsy, the Bells' young daughter, found herself attacked by a terrifying, invisible force, which pulled her hair, scratched, pinched, and even beat her.

SUDDEN DEATH

Soon the unseen force found a voice. Claiming to be an evil witch, it threw objects at members of the family. Then, it started to aim its attacks at Betsy's father, John.

On December 20, 1820, three years after the haunting began, John Bell suddenly died. A bottle of poison was found in his bedroom. The witch proudly boasted that she had caused his death.

WHAT HAPPENED NEXT?

About two months later, the haunting stopped. Since that time, many books have been written about the Bell family poltergeist. The story of the Bell Witch is still taught in Tennessee schools today.

Many rural areas of Tennessee have changed little since the days of the Bell Witch. These deserted farm buildings are on the Cumberland plateau, east of Robertson County, where the haunting took place.

FACT OR FANTASY?

When the Bell ghost began to speak, it claimed to be the "witch of old Kate Batts," a respectable elderly neighbor of the Bells who lived nearby. However, Kate Batts had no grudge against the Bell family, and John Bell never believed the story. The ghost made many other claims, all equally false.

Where was John Bell's farm?

When did the haunting begin?

Who were the main victims of the haunting?

23

When Sigmund Adam interviewed Anne-Marie Schneider for a job with his law firm in southern Germany in 1967, there seemed nothing unusual about her. But soon after she started work, Adam noticed a number of very strange things going on in the office...

GHOST FILE

Subject	The Rosenheim Poltergeist
Date	1967
Sighting	Rosenheim, Germany
Status	UNEXPLAINED

SILENT CALLS

First, there were the "silent calls," when the phones would ring and nobody would be on the line. Then, the lights started to flicker on and off. Calendars flew off the wall. Drawers shot out from desks. An oak chest slid across the floor on its own.

News of the strange events in Rosenheim soon spread. Police went to investigate, and scientists visited the office with tape recorders and cameras. But it was not until a paranormal investigator went to Rosenheim that a pattern began to emerge.

 Anne-Marie Schneider was 19 years old when she went to work in Sigmund Adam's law firm in Rosenheim.

PARANORMAL ACTIVITY

The investigator noticed that the paranormal activity occurred only when Anne-Marie Schneider was working in the office—and stopped as soon as she left the building. Interviewing her, the investigator soon found that she was an unhappy young woman, who hated her job and her boss.

FACT OR FANTASY?

The case of the Rosenheim Poltergeist still divides the experts. None of the extreme events that were said to have taken place were ever captured on film. But several scientists were convinced that what they saw was genuine—and there was no obvious sign of evidence being faked.

 Sigmund Adam displays a phone bill he received at the time of the haunting. It shows that he was charged for 600 calls to the **Time of Day** —even though all the phones in the office were out of use at the time.

THE SPIRIT DEPARTS

Soon afterward, Anne-Marie left her job—and the poltergeist left with her. But nobody could explain how a 19-year-old woman could have triggered such a storm of paranormal activity. Years later, the Rosenheim case remains one of the most bizarre and frightening of recent times.

When did the haunting begin?

How old was Anne-Marie Schneider at the time?

How did scientists try to observe the ghost?

THE KOLKATA POLTERGEIST

In December 2008, a young girl living in Kolkata, India, experienced a terrifying haunting. It started without warning—and ended as mysteriously as it began.

During the haunting, life in the family home was turned upside down and Rima found it impossible to concentrate on her schoolwork.

HAVOC

The Kolkata haunting took place in the house of a man named Ratan Das, just when his eldest daughter, Rima, was about to take an important school test.

From December 14 to 27, the poltergeist caused **havoc** in the household. Objects were moved or hidden. Members of the family were pushed and prodded by unseen forces. School books were moved, hidden, and thrown around the room. Desperate, Rima's father called the police. They were as baffled as everyone else.

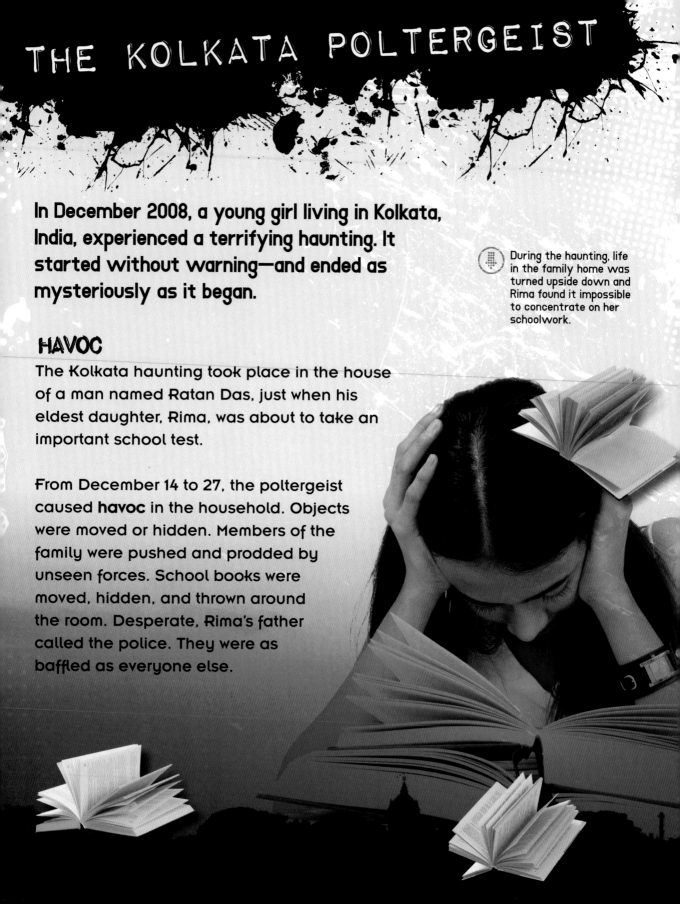

A MYSTERY UNSOLVED

In the end, no one could really explain what had happened. Was the family house triggering the paranormal activity? If so, why was the poltergeist only active when Rima was present?

Could it be that the haunting was simply linked with Rima's fears and worries about her upcoming test?

DIARY OF A HAUNTING

December 14	A vase of flowers is moved.
1December 17	Rima is pushed by invisible hands and her books are thrown around.
December 18	One of Rima's books bursts into flames.
December 20	Rima's bed catches fire.
December 21	Ratan Das calls the police.
December 22	Rima's bed and books are thrown down the stairs.
December 27	The haunting ends.

FACT OR FANTASY?

The Kolkata case centered around a young girl who was worried and anxious. Significantly, the attacks were often directed at the books that she was studying. On one occasion, a book she was reading even burst into flames.

GHOST FILE

Subject The Kolkata Poltergeist
Date December 2008
Sighting Kolkata, India
Status UNEXPLAINED

Where did the haunting take place?

How long did the haunting last?

Who was the main target of the poltergeist?

MCCONNELL'S GHOST

Some people claim that paranormal events are triggered when a person is in extreme danger or **distress**. Could this explain the **baffling** case of McConnell's ghost?

A DATE WITH DEATH

On the morning of December 7, 1918, Lieutenant David McConnell, an 18-year-old British pilot based at Scampton in Lincolnshire, UK, received orders to fly a small two-seater plane to an airfield in Tadcaster 62 miles (100 kilometers) away and return that same afternoon.

At 11:30 A.M., McConnell said goodbye to his roommate and set out for Tadcaster. He never returned. At Tadcaster airfield, his plane crashed on landing and he was killed instantly. His wristwatch, which had been broken at the instant of the crash, read 3:25 P.M.

GHOST FILE

Subject   Lieutenant David McConnell
Date   December 7, 1918
Sighting   Scampton Airfield, Lincolnshire, UK
Status   UNEXPLAINED

 World War I fighter planes were very dangerous compared to modern planes. Accidents were frequent—and often fatal.

A FAMILIAR VOICE

At the moment the plane crashed at Tadcaster, McConnell's roommate Larkin was relaxing back at the base. Hearing a familiar voice, he looked up and saw the figure of McConnell standing just a few feet away.

"Hello! Back already?"

"Yes," said the figure.

"Got there all right? Had a good trip?"

"Fine, thanks. Well, cheerio!" said the figure, and left.

WHAT HAPPENED NEXT?

When Larkin was told that McConnell had died in a crash that afternoon, he was stunned. If McConnell had died at 3:25 P.M. in Tadcaster, how could Larkin have spoken to him at exactly the same time in Scampton? Had he been dreaming?

Paranormal investigators who studied the case ruled out the possibility of a hoax. The mystery of David McConnell's ghost remains unexplained to this day.

At what time did McConnell's plane crash?

Who saw McConnell's apparition?

What did Larkin say to the apparition?

World War I pilots faced huge risks and were often very **superstitious**. But McConnell's friend Larkin was a reliable witness and had no obvious reason to make up the story.

29

THE HELPFUL HELMSMAN

In classic tales of the supernatural, ghosts and phantoms are often evil and threatening. But there are times when a supernatural presence can be a life-saver.

TROUBLE AHEAD

In July 1895, the lone yachtsman Joshua Slocum was on board his boat, *Spray*, somewhere off the coast of West Africa. Slocum was on his way to becoming the first man ever to sail around the world singlehanded. But at that moment, he was in trouble. After setting out from the Azores in the mid-Atlantic, he ran into fierce storms and was sick with severe stomach cramps.

Joshua Slocum (1844–1909) was a Canadian-American seaman and a well-known writer. His book *Alone Around the World* is a classic story of seafaring adventure.

GHOST FILE

Subject	Ghost of fifteenth-century sailor
Sighting	North Atlantic Ocean
Date	July 27, 1895
Status	UNEXPLAINED

THE GHOST PILOT

Abandoning the helm, Slocum crawled off to get some sleep. After some time below, he was getting ready to go back on deck when he was surprised to see a tall figure at the helm, dressed in the clothes of a fifteenth-century sailor.

 Joshua Slocum's sailing boat *Spray*, photographed in 1898.

FACT OR FANTASY?

Most people would say that Slocum simply imagined that he saw a ghostly sailor. Columbus was already in Slocum's thoughts, as he had read about Columbus's travels before setting out. But this does not explain how the ship stayed on course during the night.

"Señor," the **helmsman** said, "I mean you no harm. I am one of Columbus's crew, the pilot of the *Pinta*, come to aid you. Lie quiet and I will guide your ship tonight."

Slocum did as he was told. The next day, when he woke up, he found that the boat was exactly on course. He later wrote, "Columbus himself could not have held her more exactly on course. I had been in the presence of a friend and a seaman of great experience."

Where was Slocum's boat when the incident took place?

What was wrong with Slocum at the time?

Who did the ghostly sailor claim to be?

DISAPPEARANCES

THE DISAPPEARED

Here are some of the most baffling and mysterious disappearances of all time. Many of them have remained unsolved for centuries.

ASKING QUESTIONS

When people or things suddenly vanish, it is natural to ask questions —and often there is a simple explanation. Maybe a crime has been committed, or an accident of some kind has taken place.

Since the 1950s many mysterious disappearances have taken place in the area of ocean known as the Bermuda Triangle in the western North Atlantic.

But sometimes people vanish in **bizarre** circumstances, and there are no clues as to what happened—or the clues that are left behind just add to the mystery. Occasionally, an entire ship will vanish without a trace, or an aircraft will take off and never be seen again.

The British explorer Percy Fawcett disappeared in the 1920s while searching for a lost city in the jungles of Brazil.

DISTRESS SIGNALS

Usually ships or aircraft that get into trouble send out distress signals—but not always. When a DC4 airliner had trouble over Lake Michigan during a routine flight from New York to Seattle on June 23, 1950, no call for help was ever received. Debris was later found floating in the water, but the wreckage of the plane itself has never been found.

Lake Michigan has been the scene of several unexplained incidents involving ships and planes.

Just as baffling is the case of the three lighthouse keepers who disappeared on the remote Scottish island of Eilean Mohr. Inside the lighthouse, everything had been left in perfect order. The **logbook** had been kept up to date and there was no sign of anything wrong. Yet the men vanished without a trace and were never seen again.

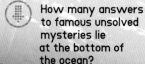

How many answers to famous unsolved mysteries lie at the bottom of the ocean?

THE LOST PATROL

Over the last 60 years, the area of ocean known as the Bermuda Triangle has been the scene of many strange disappearances. One of the most mysterious was the case of Flight 19.

 The legendary "lost squadron," Flight 19, believed lost in the Bermuda Triangle shortly after the end of World War II.

DISAPPEARANCE FILE

Subject	Flight 19
Date	December 5, 1945
Place	Coast of Florida
Status	UNEXPLAINED

LOST AT SEA

On December 5, 1945, a flight of five U.S. Avenger torpedo bombers took off from Fort Lauderdale Air Force base in Florida. The pilots were due to carry out a routine practice bombing attack at sea.

After the planes had completed the practice, the flight commander, Lieutenant Charles Carroll Taylor, exchanged several routine radio messages with the base. Then, his messages became strange and all contact was lost. The planes were never seen or heard from again.

This Avenger **torpedo** bomber is similar to the planes flown by the pilots of Flight 19. The Avenger was sturdy, easy to fly, and popular with pilots.

WHAT REALLY HAPPENED?

The truth about Flight 19 will probably never be known. The official story was that the planes were lost at sea. One theory is that unusual "magnetic forces" in the Bermuda Triangle may have interfered with compasses and other equipment on board the planes.

NO SURVIVORS

As soon as the aircraft were reported missing, a search was started. Aircraft and ships in the area were asked to look for wreckage and survivors. Nothing was ever found.

WHAT HAPPENED NEXT?

The U.S. Navy launched an investigation. It was found that after the bombing practice, the planes had headed northeast to the Bahamas, but for some reason, the flight commander had thought they were heading southwest to the Florida Keys. Instead of returning to Florida, he had in fact led the planes further out to sea. The report could not explain how he could have made such a basic mistake. It concluded with the words "Cause Unknown."

Who commanded Flight 19?

What type of plane were the pilots flying?

What were the final words of the Navy's report?

37

LOST AT SEA

When a big ship goes down, investigators can often piece together the story of what happened by studying the wreckage. But if a vessel vanishes without a trace, the mystery can remain unsolved forever.

DISAPPEARANCE FILE

Subject USS Cyclops
Date March 1918
Place North Atlantic Ocean
Status UNEXPLAINED

One such case was the *USS Cyclops*, a 17,300-ton (17,000-tonne) **cargo** ship owned by the U.S. Navy. Some time after March 4, 1918, the ship vanished while carrying a cargo of **ore** from Rio de Janeiro, Brazil to Baltimore, Maryland.

All 306 of the ship's passengers and crew disappeared without a trace. The Navy had lost warships in battle before, but it was very unusual for so many lives to be lost so mysteriously.

Some believe that the *USS Cyclops*' huge cargo of ore made her **unstable** and that she sank in a heavy storm.

DISTURBING

At the time the *Cyclops* vanished, the USA was at war with Germany. Some believed the ship could have been stolen by its German-born captain and handed over to the enemy.

After the search for the missing ship began, the U.S. Navy received a disturbing **telegram** from a U.S. official in Barbados, sent before the *Cyclops* went missing. According to the official, the ship's captain had taken on a lot of extra coal and food, as if he was preparing for a long voyage. The official also said that many of the passengers had German names. His message ended: "I fear a fate worse than sinking."

This crew member was one of 236 officers and men who are believed to have lost their lives when the USS Cyclops disappeared.

How many people were on board the USS Cyclops when it vanished?

What nationality was the ship's captain?

What was the ship carrying when it vanished?

WHAT REALLY HAPPENED?

One theory, supported by the Barbados telegram, is that German passengers took over the Cyclops, killed the crew, and sailed to Germany. But after the war ended, the Germans denied all knowledge of the ship. Many other theories have been suggested, but none that really solves the mystery.

In 1937, American pilot Amelia Earhart set out to become the first woman to fly around the world. It was a journey from which she never returned.

At 40 years old, Amelia Earhart was an outstanding pilot who had broken many flying records. Before her disappearance, both she and her navigator, Fred Noonan, had successfully completed many long flights.

EMPTY OCEAN

Just after midnight on July 2, Earhart took off from Lae, New Guinea, on one of the final stages of her journey. She was bound for Howland Island, a tiny strip of land in the middle of the Pacific, where a U.S. Coast Guard ship, the *Itasca*, was waiting to guide her in.

Early that morning, the *Itasca* picked up a radio message from Earhart saying that she could not find Howland Island. After this, the signals from Earhart's Electra 10E plane became fainter and fainter. Then, there was silence.

DISAPPEARANCE FILE

Subject	Amelia Earhart
Date	July 2, 1937
Place	Pacific Ocean
Status	UNEXPLAINED

OUT OF FUEL

At first, people thought that Earhart had run out of fuel and crashed into the ocean. Then, the radio signals were **analyzed**. One seemed to come from Gardner Island, around 310 miles (500 kilometers) south of Howland. Later, the island was searched, and a skeleton, a woman's shoe, and a piece of **aluminum**, possibly from an aircraft, were found.

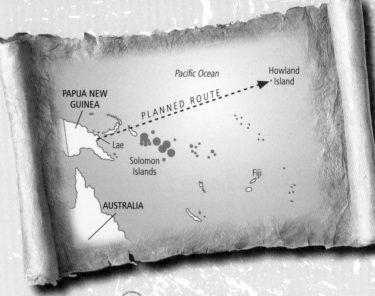

Map showing Amelia Earhart's planned route from Lae, New Guinea, to Howland Island, halfway between Australia and Hawaii.

WHAT REALLY HAPPENED?

Some have claimed that Earhart crash-landed on Japanese-occupied Saipan Island, and was later executed as a US **spy**. *However, photographs showing Earhart as a prisoner turned out to be fake. Others believe Earhart is still alive somewhere under another name, but there is no evidence to support this.*

Over the years, many theories tried to explain Amelia Earhart's disappearance, but nothing was ever found that would prove to be from her plane. Her case remains one of the greatest unsolved mysteries of the twentieth century.

What type of aircraft was Earhart flying?

Who was Earhart's navigator?

Which island was Earhart heading for when she vanished?

THE LOST COLONY

In sixteenth-century America, many **settlers** lost their lives in the struggle to build a future in the "New World." But could a whole community of 115 people really disappear without leaving any trace?

ON ROANOKE ISLAND

In 1585, English settlers arrived on Roanoke, a small island off the coast of North Carolina. They founded a **colony,** but life was hard, and the small community suffered many setbacks. When the colony's governor left and returned three years later, he was shocked to find everyone gone, the houses empty, and the paths overgrown with weeds. The only clue to what had happened was a single word, "CROATOAN," carved on a wooden post.

This reconstruction of an early English settlers' village shows how the Roanoke colony might have looked.

DISAPPEARANCE FILE

Subject	The Lost Colony of Roanoke
Date	1587
Place	Roanoke Island, North Carolina
Status	UNEXPLAINED

WHAT REALLY HAPPENED?

*One possibility is that the settlers ran out of food, tried to return to England, but died on the journey. More likely, the survivors ended up living among nearby Native American tribes, who either adopted or **enslaved** them. Scientists and historians are debating this theory.*

"CROATOAN"

Before he left, the governor told the settlers that if anything went wrong, they were to leave a clue to what had happened or where they went. If they were attacked or driven out against their will, they were to carve a cross on a tree.

For years afterward, people tried to find out what happened. Some reported seeing fair-skinned people on nearby Croatoan Island. Others reported seeing traces of settlements further along the North Carolina coast. To this day, no one knows for sure what happened to the Roanoke settlers.

Archaeologists **excavate** the site of a fort close to where the original Roanoke colony is believed to have stood.

When was the Roanoke colony founded?

How many colonists disappeared?

What word was found carved on a post at Roanoke?

THE LINER THAT VANISHED

On July 26, 1909, the luxury steamer SS *Waratah* set sail from Durban, South Africa, with 211 passengers and crew. Built to carry passengers emigrating from Europe to Australia, the *Waratah* was returning to England after her second voyage.

BRIGHT FLASHES

On July 27, a ship called the *Harlow* spotted a large steamer that looked like the *Waratah* some distance away. Later, the crew of the *Harlow* saw two bright flashes on the horizon, but they thought they were caused by fires on the shore.

The *Waratah* was due to reach Cape Town on July 29. She never arrived. Naval ships searched the area where she was last seen, but no trace of the ship was ever found.

 Known as the "Australian *Titanic*," the SS *Waratah* was only one year old at the time of her disappearance. The ship did not carry a radio, but this was not unusual at the time.

DISAPPEARANCE FILE

Subject	SS Waratah
Date	July 27, 1909
Place	Indian Ocean
Status	UNEXPLAINED

PUBLIC INQUIRY

After the *Waratah* disappeared, a public inquiry was held in London. Some experts said the ship might have been top-heavy; others said she could have been the victim of a freak wave or a "hole in the ocean," where winds and currents can drag even a large ship to the bottom.

Many theories were argued back and forth. The well-known writer of the *Sherlock Holmes* stories, Sir Arthur Conan Doyle, even held a **séance** to try and find out what happened. But in the end, no one could explain how such a large ship could vanish without leaving either wreckage or survivors.

WHAT REALLY HAPPENED?

The *Waratah* was carrying a heavy cargo of lead which could have shifted, causing her to capsize. But if so, where was the wreck? In 1999, the wreck of a big ship was spotted in the area where the *Waratah* vanished, but this was found to be a transport ship sunk by a German **U-boat** in 1942.

Many ships have been lost in stormy seas off this rocky **headland**, known as the Cape of Good Hope, on the southern tip of South Africa.

How many people were on board the *Waratah*?

What famous ship was the *Waratah* compared to?

Which port was the *Waratah* bound for?

THE MARY CELESTE

In 1872, a small cargo ship was found drifting in the Atlantic Ocean. Everything on board seemed perfectly normal, except for one thing: the ship was deserted. No trace of the crew has ever been found. The case of the *Mary Celeste* remains one of the great unsolved sea mysteries of all time.

SHIP OF GHOSTS

On November 5, 1872, the *Mary Celeste* set sail from New York bound for Genoa, Italy with a valuable cargo of raw alcohol. On board were Captain Benjamin Briggs, his wife and daughter, plus a crew of seven men.

Ten days later, another ship, the *Dei Gratia*, set sail on a similar route under Captain David Morehouse, an acquaintance of Briggs. After a month at sea, Morehouse spotted the *Mary Celeste* drifting in the Atlantic. He immediately sensed that something was wrong and sent his **chief mate**, Oliver Deveau, to investigate. Finding the *Mary Celeste* deserted, Deveau and two others sailed her to Gibraltar.

In a final letter to his mother, the captain of the *Mary Celeste*, Benjamin Briggs, wrote: "Our vessel is in beautiful trim and I hope we shall have a fine passage."

WHAT HAPPENED NEXT?

In Gibraltar, an official inquiry was held. The crew of the *Dei Gratia* was questioned and the *Mary Celeste* was examined. All of the crew's clothes and possessions were still on board. The cargo was intact. The hatch on the main cargo **hold** was closed, but two smaller hatches were open. The last entry in the log was dated November 25.

 A painting of the *Mary Celeste* in 1861. At this time, the ship was named the *Amazon*.

WHAT REALLY HAPPENED?

Over the years many people have tried to solve the mystery of the Mary Celeste. Some even claim the crew were abducted by aliens! One theory is that alcohol fumes from the cargo may have made the captain think the vessel was about to explode, and this was why he and the crew left in such a hurry.

The inquiry found that Captain Briggs and his crew had abandoned the *Mary Celeste* in a great hurry and taken to the **lifeboat**. Why they left the ship and what happened to them afterward still remains a mystery.

Who was the captain of the Mary Celeste?

What cargo was the Mary Celeste carrying?

Who boarded the Mary Celeste when she was found?

THE LOST ARMY OF CAMBYSES

In the summer of 2000, scientists searching for oil in the Egyptian desert came across weapons, jewelry, and human bones buried in the sand. Could these be the remains of the lost army of Cambyses?

After crossing the Sinai desert, Cambyses' army swept into Egypt, easily defeating the forces of Psamtik III at the Battle of Pelusium.

A MIGHTY RULER

In the sixth century BCE, the Persian ruler Cambyses II was one of the most powerful men in the ancient world. After successfully invading Egypt in 525 BCE, Cambyses sent an army of 50,000 soldiers from Thebes to Siwa in the desert west of the Nile River. The soldiers' orders were to attack the Temple of Amun, where rebel priests were refusing to accept his rule.

After marching for seven days across the desert, the army was resting at an **oasis** when a fierce wind sprang up. Soon columns of whirling sand descended on the troops, burying men and animals in clouds of dust.

DISAPPEARANCE FILE

Name	The Lost Army of Cambyses
Date	525 or 524 BCE
Place	Western Egyptian Desert
Status	UNEXPLAINED

The story of Cambyses' army was first told by the Greek historian Herodotus (484 –425 BCE).

WHAT HAPPENED NEXT?

Hearing what had happened, Cambyses sent out riders to try to find his army. The trail led through the desert oasis of Bahariya, then southwest toward Siwa, but disappeared in the sand. The huge army had vanished without a trace.

For many years, historians thought the story was just a **myth**. But over the last ten years, important finds have been made in Egypt's western desert. These are now being studied by experts. Many believe they could hold the answer to the mysterious fate of Cambyses' army.

Remains of the ancient temple of Amun at Siwa, in the western Egyptian desert.

WHAT REALLY HAPPENED?

Over the years many explorers and archaeologists have searched in vain for traces of Cambyses' army. The remains found in Egypt recently seem to be of Persian origin and appear to belong to soldiers who became lost or stranded in the desert. Whether they belong to Cambyses' army is less certain.

When did Cambyses invade Egypt?

Which temple was Cambyses' army planning to attack?

Where have remains of an army been discovered?

THE VANISHING LIGHTHOUSEMEN

Eilean Mohr off the west coast of Scotland is one of the most remote islands in the British Isles. According to local legend, it was haunted by ghosts who were determined to drive out intruders. Could this explain the mysterious case of the vanishing lighthouse keepers?

 Eilean Mohr is the largest of the seven rocky Flannan Isles. It rises 282 feet (87 meters) above the Atlantic Ocean, on the west coast of Scotland.

DISAPPEARANCE FILE

Names	James Ducat, Thomas Marshall, and Donald McArthur
Date	December 1900
Place	Eilean Mohr, Scotland
Status	UNEXPLAINED

DESERTED

On December 26, 1900, lighthouse keeper Joseph Moore was returning to Eilean Mohr by boat after a two-week leave. As Moore approached the island and looked for the usual signs of welcome, he was puzzled to see that there was nobody waiting at the **landing stage** to greet him.

Inside the lighthouse, Moore found the living quarters deserted. On the kitchen table were the remains of a half-eaten meal. An upturned chair lay on the floor. The lighthouse was empty, and its three occupants had disappeared without trace.

WHAT HAPPENED NEXT?

Alarmed, Moore returned with four others to make a full investigation. They discovered that two of the keepers must have left the lighthouse dressed for stormy weather. A third set of **oilskins** was still hanging on the hook.

The west landing stage had been lashed by gales. A lifebelt had been ripped from its mountings. But no trace was found of the lighthouse keepers, nor any sign of what could have happened to them. To this day, the mystery of their disappearance remains unsolved.

The job of the lighthouse keepers was to keep the lamp lit to guide ships away from the rocks at night.

WHAT REALLY HAPPENED?

Some claim that the three men were carried off by a giant bird or sea creature. It is more likely that during a storm, two of the men went to check the crane on the west landing. Meanwhile, the third man saw big waves approaching and rushed out to warn them. In the confusion, all three were swept out to sea.

When were the disappearances discovered?

Who discovered the disappearances?

How many men disappeared?

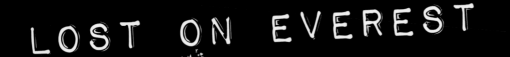

DISAPPEARANCE FILE

Names   George Mallory
             Andrew Irvine
Date   June 8, 1924
Place   Mount Everest, Nepal
Status   SOLVED

At the time of his disappearance, Mallory was 38 years old and had many years' experience as a mountaineer. Both he and Irvine were well equipped for climbing at high **altitude**.

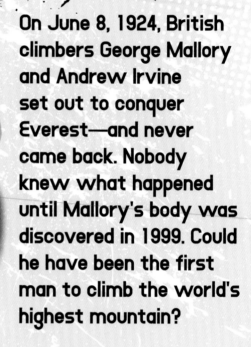

On June 8, 1924, British climbers George Mallory and Andrew Irvine set out to conquer Everest—and never came back. Nobody knew what happened until Mallory's body was discovered in 1999. Could he have been the first man to climb the world's highest mountain?

IN SIGHT OF VICTORY

On the day that Mallory and Irvine made their fateful attempt on the **summit** of Everest, thick clouds hid the mountain. But for a few minutes around lunchtime, the cloud lifted, and the two men were spotted within sight of the summit. Then, they were once more hidden from view. It was the last time they were seen alive.

At 29,029 feet (8,848 meters), Mount Everest in the Himalayas is the world's highest mountain.

WHAT REALLY HAPPENED?

Many believe that Mallory's attempt on the summit of Everest was successful, and that he died on the way down the mountain. However, there is no proof of this. The fact that the photograph of his wife was not found on his person when his body was discovered in 1999 does not prove that he reached the summit.

MEMORIAL

When Mallory and Irvine failed to come back, their friends waited several days. Then, accepting that they both must have died on the mountain, they built a memorial **cairn** and left. The mystery of what really happened that day, and whether the two men reached the summit, has never been solved.

These snow goggles, pocket knife, and watch were found on Mallory's body in 1999.

WHAT HAPPENED NEXT?

In 1933, Irvine's ice axe was found on a slope at 27,600 feet (8,500 meters), but there was no sign of his body. It was not until 1999 that Mallory's frozen remains were found 850 feet (300 meters) further down the slope.

Rope marks showed that Mallory had fallen, been caught by the rope, and then fallen again. A photo of his wife that he planned to leave on the summit was not in his pocket. Many people took this as a sign that Mallory and Irvine had reached the summit that day and that they were on the way down when the accident occurred.

On what date did Mallory set out for the summit?

When was Mallory's body found?

What did Mallory plan to leave on the summit?

INTO THE UNKNOWN

DISAPPEARANCE FILE

Subject Percy Fawcett
Date June 1925
Place Mato Grosso, Brazil
Status UNEXPLAINED

In 1925, the well-known British explorer Percy Fawcett disappeared in mysterious circumstances during an expedition to find an ancient lost city in the jungles of Brazil. His fate and that of his son Jack is still unknown.

LOST CITY

Fawcett was convinced that an ancient lost city that he called "Z" existed somewhere in the Mato Grosso, a vast wooded region in western Brazil. He left behind strict instructions that, if he did not return, no one should try to rescue him in case they went missing, too.

The legendary explorer Percy Fawcett was said to be the inspiration for the film character Indiana Jones.

On May 29, 1925, Fawcett sent a message to his wife that he had reached the Xingu River and was about to enter unexplored territory. The message ended: "You need have no fear of failure." Shortly after this, he headed north into the rainforest. Neither he nor his son Jack was ever seen again.

Atlantic Ocean
VENEZUELA
Amazon River
Mato Grosso
Xingu River
PERU
BOLIVIA
BRAZIL
Pacific Ocean

Map showing the Amazon Basin and the Xingu River region, where Percy Fawcett and his son Jack were last seen.

RUMORS

After Fawcett disappeared, many rumors started to go around. Some said that Fawcett had been killed by tribespeople or wild animals; others said that Fawcett had lost his memory and was living among **cannibals**.

An explorer named Orlando Villas Boas claimed that Kalapalo tribespeople had confessed to murdering Fawcett and had handed the body over to him. But the bones were later found not to be Fawcett's.

In an interview in 1998, an elder of the Kalapalo denied that the tribe had had any part in Fawcett's death. More than 80 years later, the mystery of his disappearance is as baffling as ever.

WHAT REALLY HAPPENED?

For a long time, it was thought that Fawcett had been murdered by tribespeople of the Upper Xingu River. But Fawcett took care to stay on friendly terms with local people and always took gifts for them. It is most likely that he simply got lost or died of natural causes in the jungle.

 The Mato Grosso region of Brazil has often been visited by explorers searching for lost cities.

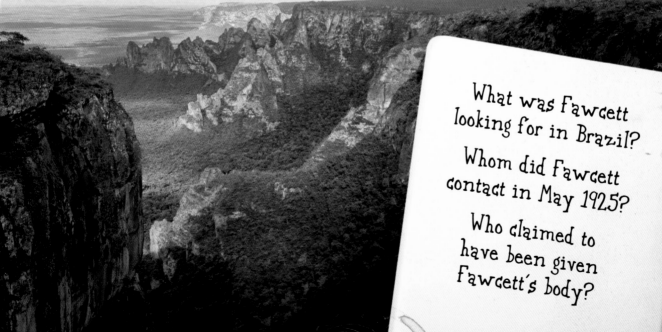

What was Fawcett looking for in Brazil?

Whom did Fawcett contact in May 1925?

Who claimed to have been given Fawcett's body?

THE LOST WORLD OF THE MAYA

Between 250 CE and 900 CE, Central America was home to one of the greatest civilizations the world has ever known. The huge stone buildings of the Mayan people mysteriously crumbled and their cities were reclaimed by the jungle. What happened?

DISAPPEARANCE FILE

Subject	Mayan Civilization
Date	780 CE onward, cities abandoned
Place	Central America
Status	UNEXPLAINED

A THRIVING CIVILIZATION

 Mayan texts have been found inscribed on stone monuments and pottery. Some texts were also painted on a type of paper made from tree bark.

Mayan civilization thrived for nearly 2,000 years. The Mayans were great builders, mathematicians, and scientists. From **observatories** like the one at Chichen Itza, in Mexico, they even tracked the movements of the planets. Then, something happened that turned their world upside down.

About 780 CE, the Mayan cities were suddenly abandoned. It was as if the inhabitants had left and never returned. When people learned to read Mayan symbols in the 1970s, experts hoped the inscriptions would explain what had happened. They did not.

FAMINE AND DROUGHT

The mysterious decline of the great Mayan civilization has always puzzled historians. Several Mayan cities have been excavated, but no signs of warfare or violent conflict have ever been found.

For a long time it was believed that a terrible sickness killed the population, or that a disease killed off their crops and caused the people to starve. Recently, it has been suggested that the Mayans suffered a catastrophic drought that caused **famine** and loss of life on a large scale.

WHAT REALLY HAPPENED?

It now seems very likely that a large-scale drought caused the sudden collapse of the Mayan world. Scientists have looked at soil samples taken from Mexico's Lake Chichancanab. These show that in the ninth century when Mayan civilization disappeared, the region was at its driest in 7,000 years.

The Kukulkan Pyramid at Chichen Itza is one of the most important surviving remnants of Mayan civilization. Like all Mayan structures, it was built by armies of laborers without the help of machines or metal tools.

Where was the lost world of the Maya?

When did the Mayan civilization collapse?

When did people first learn to read Mayan symbols?

THE SHIP THAT WOULDN'T DIE

In the 1920s, the SS *Baychimo* was a small cargo steamer that sailed around the northern coast of Canada, delivering supplies and trading furs with local people. Then, one cold day in 1931, the Arctic ice closed in. The *Baychimo* was trapped!

ARCTIC RESCUE

Realizing he and his crew were in danger, the captain radioed for help. Soon after, the first-ever **airlift** from the Arctic took place. Twenty-two of the ship's crew were rescued. The rest decided to shelter nearby for the winter and reboard the ship in the spring when the ice melted.

Since the *Baychimo* first drifted free of the ice, people have managed to board her several times, but nobody ever succeeded in rescuing her or towing her safely back to harbor.

DISAPPEARANCE FILE

Subject	SS *Baychimo*
Date	November 24, 1931
Place	Arctic Ocean
Status	UNEXPLAINED

It never happened. After a severe blizzard in late November, the crew emerged from their wooden huts to find that the pack ice had loosened—and the *Baychimo* had floated away!

GHOST SHIP

Since then, the *Baychimo* has often been spotted drifting across the Arctic Ocean. In 1932, an explorer sighted her while sledding across the Arctic. The next year, Inuit hunters saw the ship and boarded her but had to leave when they saw a storm approaching. In September 1935 and November 1939, the ship was spotted again near Wainwright, Alaska.

In 1962, another group of Inuit people sighted her on the Beaufort Sea.

 Inuit people live throughout the Canadian and Arctic regions where the *Baychimo* has been seen.

The last recorded sighting was in 1969—38 years after the *Baychimo* had first been abandoned.

In the early 1990s, the company that originally owned the *Baychimo* was unable to say whether the little ship was still afloat. Perhaps she is still adrift somewhere in the Arctic…

WHAT REALLY HAPPENED?

The Arctic Ocean has a pattern of circular currents that are driven by wind and by oceanic flows. These flows come in via the Bering Straits and the Greenland Sea. Once the Baychimo was caught in these unpredictable currents, it could have drifted in and out of inhabited areas, ending up almost anywhere.

What type of ship was the *Baychimo*?

When was the *Baychimo* last seen?

When did the *Baychimo* first become trapped in the ice?

GLOSSARY

Airlift An operation to rescue people by plane or helicopter.

Altitude Height above sea level.

Aluminum A type of metal.

Analyze To examine something very carefully.

Apparition A visible presence of a ghostly person or thing.

Baffling Hard to explain, puzzling.

Bizarre Strange or unusual.

Cairn A pile of stones built as a landmark or to mark a grave.

Cannibals Tribal people who eat the flesh of humans for food or as part of a ritual.

Caretaker A person who looks after a place or building.

Cargo Goods carried on a ship.

Chief mate A senior officer on board a ship.

Colony A community of settlers.

Curator A person who is in charge of a museum or collection.

Curse To wish harm upon a person or thing.

Death mask A wax or plaster cast of a dead person's face.

Distress When somebody is worried, upset, or in trouble.

Electromagnetic A type of energy sometimes said to be released by ghosts and poltergeists.

Enslave To force a person to work very hard without being paid.

Excavate To dig up remains of a civilization.

Famine A time when there is not enough food to eat.

Fiction A story that is made up by a writer.

Fiesta A Spanish word for a type of party or carnival.

Flagstone A stone slab used for paving or flooring.

Forecastle The part of a sailing ship where the crew have their quarters.

Genuine True, real, or based on fact.

Hallucination A vision or sound of something that is not really there.

Havoc Chaos and confusion.

Headland A piece of land that sticks out into the ocean.

Helmsman A person who steers a ship or sailing boat.

Hoax A deliberate trick or deception.

Hold The part of a ship where the cargo is stored.

Intruder Someone who enters a building without permission.

Landing stage A place where a ship or boat can tie up safely.

Legend An old story that has often been told, but may or may not be true.

Lifeboat A vessel that passengers and crew members can use to escape from a sinking ship.

Logbook A written record of events.

Memorial A stone or statue in memory of a person who has died.

Miracle An amazing event that cannot be explained.

Myth (a) An ancient story, often about gods or heroes; (b) a story that is found not to be true.

Oasis A fertile area in the desert where water can be found.

Observatory A building from which scientists can study the night sky.

Oilskin A type of thick, waterproof jacket.

Ore Raw material from which metals can be extracted.

Pact A deal or agreement.

Paranormal Contrary to the laws of science.

Patriotic Devoted to your country.

Plaque A memorial stone or plate.

Poltergeist A ghost that is invisible, but can make objects move around.

Séance A meeting where people try to make contact with the spirits of dead people.

Settler A person who goes to start a new life in another country.

Summit The highest point of a mountain.

Supernatural Unable to be explained by science.

Superstitious Putting too much trust in ideas which are not based on reason.

Telegram A type of message that is sent by telephone wires but is delivered in printed form.

Torpedo A missile that travels through water and can be launched from the air.

U-boat A German submarine.

Unstable Unbalanced, liable to tip over.

GHOSTS ANSWERS

Page

8-9   Queen Wilhelmina of the Netherlands; 1865; "You have me at a disadvantage, Sir!"

10-11   On the battlements of the Tower; Henry VIII; the nephews of Richard III.

12-13   1841; Ned Kelly; 1972.

14-15   South Africa; Officer Maxwell; the library's former caretaker, Robert Thomas.

16-17   Mons; April 24, 1915; Arthur Machen.

18-19   1676; Van der Decken; George V.

20-21   RGN; Villa Camila Park; a projection of a photograph of a girl.

22-23   Adams, Tennessee; 1817; John Bell and his daughter, Betsy.

24-25   1967; 19; with tape recorders and cameras.

26-27   At the home of Ratan Das in Kolkata, India; from December 14 to 27, 2008; Rima Das.

28-29   3:25 P.M.; McConnell's roommate, Larkin; "Hello! Back already?"

30-31   In the north Atlantic, somewhere off the west coast of Africa; he was sick with severe stomach cramps; the pilot of Columbus's ship the Pinta.